IN THE CAIRNGORMS

Also by Nan Shepherd

The Quarry Wood
The Weatherhouse
A Pass In The Grampians

The Living Mountain

Wild Geese

IN THE CAIRNGORMS

Nan Shepherd

Foreword
by
Robert Macfarlane

Illustrations by June Allan

G

Galileo Publishers, Cambridge

Galileo Publishers
16 Woodlands Road
Great Shelford
Cambridge CB22 5LW
UK

www.galileopublishing.co.uk

Distributed in the USA by:
SCB Distributors
15608 S. New Century Drive
Gardena, CA 90248-2129

ISBN 978-1-912916-13-9

First published in 1934 by The Moray Press
This new hardback edition published 2019
© 2019 The Estate of Nan Shepherd
Foreword © 2014, 2019 Robert Macfarlane
Illustrations © 2014 June Allan
Cover photo Robert Hyde

1

All rights reserved. This book is sold subject to the condition that it shall not, by way of trade or otherwise, be lent, resold, hired out or otherwise circulated in any form of binding or cover other than that in in which it is published and without a similar condition including this condition being imposed on the subsequent purchaser.

Printed in the EU

To
Betty and John MacMurray

"Islands are united by the bottom of the sea"

CONTENTS

FOREWORD by Robert Macfarlane   IX

IN THE CAIRNGORMS   Page

I	Singing Burn	1
II	Above Loch Avon	2
III	Loch Avon	2
IV	Images of beauty	3
V	Fires	4
VI	And if upon the angry height	6
VII	The Hill	7
VIII	The Hill Burns	8
IX	The three great rocks	10
X	The Bush	11
XI	Lux Perpetua	12
XII	Strange gifts of pleasure	14
XIII	Tread not in the planets' places	15
XIV	Blackbird in Snow	16
XV	Summit of Corrie Etchachan	18
XVI	Its own most lovely wraith	19
XVII	Quiet over Lochnagar	20
XVIII	Caul', caul' as the wall	21
XIX	Fawn	22
XX	Spring	23
XXI	The Flooded Meads	23
XXII	Flood	24
XXIII	Pool beside the Birches	25
XXIV	Day without Sun	26
XXV	A Girl in Love	27
XXVI	Embodiment	28
XXVII	O licht amo' the hills	30

OTHER LYRICS

Crusoe	33
The Man who journeyed to his Heart's Desire	34
Winter Branches	35

Astonishment is in the Skies	36
Creation of an Earth	37
A Dead Love	38
Without Expiation	39
Ptolemaic System of Love	40

FOURTEEN YEARS

Snow	43
La Vita Nuova	44
Half Love	45
In Separation	46
Without my Right	47
Love Eternal	48
An Ecstasy remembered	49
Growth	50
Pardon	51
Not in a Glass	52
Real Presence	53

OTHER POEMS

Achiltibuie	57
Next Morning	58
On a Still Morning	59
Rhu Coigach	60
Falketind	61
The Trees	62
Underground	63
The Dryad	64
Arthur's Seat	65
The Burning Glass	66
Union	67
Street Urchins	68

NOTES TO THE FOREWORD   71

FOREWORD

by Robert Macfarlane

The first two lines of *In The Cairngorms* catch much of the book's strange magic: 'Oh burnie with the glass-white shiver, / Singing over stone'. What a start it is—at once homely and eerie, pitched somewhere between lullaby and cantrip. Out of the water's stone-song springs Nan's own quick lyric. I have read those lines a dozen times or more, and they send a glass-white shiver down my spine on each new occasion. The tiny poem of which they are part still haunts my ear; I hear it when I am in the hills.

Nan Shepherd (1893–1981) is now best-known for her prose non-fiction masterpiece *The Living Mountain*, written in the 1940s but not published until 1977, shortly before her death. In her lifetime though, she was most famous as a novelist of the Scottish Renaissance: between 1928 and 1933 she published three novels—*The Quarry Wood*, *The Weatherhouse* and *A Pass in The Grampians*—set in small communities in north-east Scotland, and all concerned with strong young women making their way against the current of convention. But the book of which Shepherd herself seems to have been most proud was a volume of poems, *In The Cairngorms*, published in 1934 in a handsome green and sable hardback by the Moray Press of Edinburgh. The print run was small and the book was not reprinted—until now, eighty years after its first appearance.

Poetry was, to Shepherd, the purest of forms. At its best it held 'in intensest being the very heart of all experience', she wrote to her friend and fellow writer Neil Gunn, and offered glimpses of the 'burning heart of all life'.[1] She began to write verse as a teenager, and published several poems in the Aberdeen University student magazine, *Alma Mater*, while an undergraduate. Poetry never came easily to Shepherd: she felt that she could only produce it when 'possess[ed]', such that her 'whole nature … suddenly leaped into life'. This happened rarely: it took her a quarter of a century to gather the forty-six poems of *In The Cairngorms*. It was to be her only collection of poetry. Despite taking such patient care over the book's creation, she was dissatisfied with it, worrying aloud to Gunn that her poetry—'about stars and mountains and light'—was too 'cold', too 'inhuman'.[2]

It is true that her poems are 'cold', but they are not chilly and they are certainly not inhuman. Shepherd's great subject as a writer across all genres was the inter-animating relationship of mind and matter. She was exhilarated by evidence of the earth's vast indifference to human consciousness (the mindless 'granites and schists' of the Cairngorms, and the streamwater of the plateau that 'does nothing, absolutely nothing, but be itself').[3] But she also believed, like the Wordsworth of *The Prelude*, that sustained contemplation of outer landscapes led—at last, after 'toil'—to a subtler understanding of the 'spirit'. In the Cairngorms, therefore, she came to feel 'not out of myself, but in myself'; the final 'grace' accorded by the mountains she loved was a deepened knowledge of 'Being'.[4] This doubled motion—the exploratory movement out into wild landscape simultaneous with the confirming movement back into the self—lends these poems their uncanny atmosphere: the hills are both hostile and habitual, unsettling and enfolding. This uncanniness is keenest in the four short lyrics written in the Doric (the north-east dialect of Scots) that stud in the book like garnets in granite. Here Shepherd shows herself compelled by what she elsewhere called 'the recesses'[5] or interior aspects of the massif: the 'deepmaist pit' of Loch Avon, into whose deep and lucid waters—('Bricht, an bricht, an bricht as air')—the poem glances; or a stone wall buried under snowdrifts on remote Ben a' Bhuird.

Shepherd's prose—like that of J.A. Baker, author of *The Peregrine* (1967)—trembled often on the brink of poetry, and her poetry on the brink of prose. It is fascinating to watch her testing out images, tropes and incidents in these poems that would later find re-expression in *The Living Mountain*. The impossible blue peak seen distantly in 'The Hill' and 'Pardon' appears again on the second page of *The Living Mountain*: 'I could have sworn I saw a shape, distinct and blue, very clear and small, further off than any hill the chart recorded.'[6] The water of 'The Hill Burns' that flows 'like some pure essence of being, Invisible in itself, / seen only by its movement' resurges in Shepherd's dazzling prose passages on the Wells of Dee. The Doric gaze into the 'pit' of Loch Avon is reworked as her near-fall over a submarine 'gulf of brightness so profound that the mind stopped', while bathing naked in the loch with a friend.[7] The paradox of 'The Summit of Coire Etchachan'—how can a 'corrie' have a 'summit'?—becomes one of the key concepts of *The Living Mountain*: that mountains should be understood in terms of their hollows, absences and transparencies, such that one walks 'into' them rather than merely 'up' or 'over' them.

There are also, of course, aspects of the poems that have their counterparts nowhere else, such as the beautiful 'Blackbird In Snow', in which a seemingly 'infinite' song spills from a blackbird's 'small perishable throat' (another iteration of Shepherd's interest in volume that exceeds its containment). Not all of the poems are, it must be said, successful. Shepherd excels at a sparse boreal grammar—the 'snow driving dim on the blast', or a winter sky that is 'green as ice'—and is less good when trying out a tone of hyperbolic *sturm-und-drang* (the 'Destroying Angel' that smites men in 'Image of Beauty') or hints of symbolist feyness: dreams of gazing 'through … enchanted air' to witness 'the form of the unseen'. These are already vestigial traces though—of high Romanticism and late-Victorian symbolism respectively—and by the time of *The Living Mountain*, she would have purged all such relics.

An extraordinary studio portrait exists of Shepherd as a young woman. Her chin is tilted up, and she stares out of the top right of the frame, as if at a far-off prospect of hills. She is wearing a brocaded blouse and a broad head-band with a jewel set into its centre. Her hair is parted down the middle and thick glossy plaits tumble either side to her waist. The overall appearance is faintly Native American, without any implication of parody or foolish fancy-dress. She is a charismatic presence: strong, bold-eyed and strikingly beautiful. This is the Shepherd who was remembered by a fellow undergraduate as 'a tall slim figure with a halo of chestnut plaits, a Blessed Damozel expression and an awe-inspiring dispatch case'.[8] That 'dispatch case' was evidence of her commitment to study. She was shaped by the teaching of Herbert Grierson, the first Professor of English Literature at the University of Aberdeen, a 'long lean man' who 'spoke like a torrent'. It was Grierson who led her, she later recalled, 'to understand how minute, precise and particularised knowledge had to be, and then [to see] to our delight that it need not cease to exhilarate'[9]—an allegiance to 'precise' and 'particularised' knowledge would become an insignia of Shepherd's own 'exhilarating' work.

Like Martha Ironside, the heroine of her first novel *The Quarry Wood* (1928), Shepherd 'coveted knowledge and willingly suffered privations in the pursuit of learning',[10] and among those privations were the hardships of hill-walking (the toil, the cold, the rain), for to Shepherd walking was inextricable from 'learning'. It was by walking 'into the Cairngorms' that she developed and refined her philosophy. Her relationship with the massif was life-long. She lived for eighty-eight years in the same house in the Deeside village of Cults (now a suburb of Aberdeen). 'I have had the same bedroom all my life!', she once said, gladly.[11] The foothills of the Cairngorms rose away to the west, and from an early age she explored the range. After graduating from Aberdeen in 1915, she was appointed to the staff of the Aberdeen Training Centre for Teachers, where she became a full-time lecturer in 1919, and from which she retired at last in 1956. During her decades as a teacher of teachers, she would take students and friends out into the Cairngorms: to a howff above Braemar on the side of Morrone, which served as a base for exploring the southern reaches of the range, and to a shepherd's bothy north of the Lairig Ghru which was equipped with camp beds and sleeping bags.

Shepherd was, the novelist Jessie Kesson recalled, 'reticent about herself'. She possessed a 'grace of the soul' that expressed itself in part as discretion.[12] But she was also a person of passions. She lived with a zeal that the controlled prose of *The Living Mountain* can sometimes disguise—but which is forcefully in evidence in her poems. Reading all forty-six poems in order, a sensibility springs to life: intense, rapturous, intellectually committed and elementally inspired, loving and sometimes troubled. 'Strange gifts of pleasure has the mind, / Strange darknesses the soul', reflects the speaker of one.

These 'strange darknesses' are most apparent in the concluding sequence of sonnets, 'Fourteen Years' (which curiously limits itself to eleven poems). Encountering these poems after the high-altitude abstractions of the first two-thirds of the collection is a shock. They are raw, vexed and yawing in their tones. The sequence recounts the humiliations and injuries of a lover: someone 'broken and spent with loving … /

with half-fulfilled desire', the victim of 'Black self-knowledge, eating like a curse'. In their pitched horrors they recall George Meredith's devastating sonnet sequence *Modern Love*, which so shook the Victorian ideal of marriage. If they can be said to have a positive movement, it is perhaps towards a theology of matter, in which human love is subsumed into a radiant materialism of 'amazed beatitude'. The darkest of them by far is 'Without My Right', a sonnet in which the speaker yearns to 'infect' a sleeping lover with his or her 'being', thus prosecuting a form of ontological 'rape'. It is an extraordinary text, which by its very subject issues a warning against coercive interpretation.

So we must be wary of identifying the speaker of these 'bruised and oblique' sonnets as Shepherd herself.[13] Yet it is clear that she used them in some way to dramatise personal experience. 'Very few people understand them', said Shepherd of the poems late in her life, 'which makes me feel better', and she alluded to—though did not name—a 'man for whom some of the sonnets were written'.[14] Shepherd never married. Persistent posthumous rumours have linked her romantically to Rupert Brooke, but there is no evidence that they even met. Her most prolonged relationship was platonic and dutiful: with Mary Lawson, known as 'Mamie', who at the age of sixteen became housekeeper for the Shepherds. Mamie, who had 'a soul of gold and a tongue that would clip clouts',[15] stayed with the family until her death at ninety-two in 1973. Towards the end of Mamie's life, in a reversal of roles, Shepherd became her devoted carer, regardless of the demands it made on her own ageing body. Despite her lack of partners, though, Shepherd was neither repressed or prudish. One friend remarked that 'Nan was inimitable with a tale that was a little earthy',[16] and when in 2011 I spoke to a former student of Shepherd's, she remembered Shepherd's refreshing candour about sex, and especially her refusal to teach a bowdlerised version of *Tess of the D'Urbervilles*.

Shepherd's 'lust' was at last for 'mountain tops',[17] as she put it, and her hunger for sensuous gratification found its bodily if not erotic fulfilment in the hills. This was a philosophical declaration as well as a personal one, for Shepherd belonged to a tradition of thought that runs from Locke via Kant to the phenomenology of Edmund Husserl and Maurice Merleau-Ponty. Like Kant, she developed a participatory model of perception, in which the sense-data of the material world is animated into knowledge by the mind's categories of understanding. But where Kant only grudgingly admitted the body to his epistemology, for Shepherd the body was vital to apprehension. She lived, as she once put it, 'all the way through', relishing the touch, feel, sight, scent and sounds of the world.[18]

Writing of the poet Charles Murray—the man who seems most likely to have been the addressee of the 'Fourteen Years' sonnets—Shepherd attributed the 'striking power' of his poetry to the fact that 'he said yes to life'.[19] So did she, and the power of her writing is also born of this affirmative gusto. Jessie Kesson once asked Shepherd if she believed in an afterlife. 'I hope it is true for those who have had a lean life', she replied, 'For myself—this has been so good, so fulfilling.'[20]

Shepherd did have an afterlife, of course—and an extraordinary one. In the past decade especially, as her novels, prose and poetry have found their ways back into print and into the hearts and hands of a new generation of readers, she has become one of the most influential of twentieth-century Scottish writers. Countless contemporary artists, photographers, musicians, nature writers, feminists, mountaineers, film-makers, historians, ecologists, philosophers, cartographers and everyday walkers and readers have responded with passion and imagination to Shepherd's vision. Graduate students toil over dissertations on Shepherd's works and beat a path to her literary archive in Edinburgh. The 'studio portrait' I described earlier can now be found on the Royal Bank of Scotland £5 note, folded into millions of wallets and pockets across Scotland, accompanied by an image of the Cairngorms themselves, and a line from *The Living Mountain*. And an excellent biography of Shepherd has been written by Charlotte Peacock—who in the course of her research brought to light twelve new poems by Shepherd, which are included here in this new edition of *In The Cairngorms*, including the luminous 'Achiltibuie'. What would Shepherd have made of all this, I sometimes wonder? The bank-note, the biography, the experimental in situ dance-interpretations? I imagine her giving a quiet wise smile, a slight shake of the head—and then turning to walk away up a long path through heather and rock, leading towards distant, low-slung hills.

Cambridge, December 2013 & August 2019

IN THE CAIRNGORMS

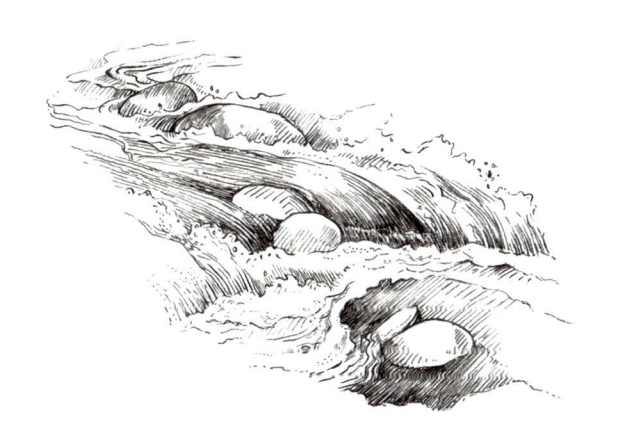

I

Singing Burn

O burnie with the glass-white shiver,
Singing over stone,
So quick, so clear, a hundred year
Singing one song alone,
From crystal sources fed forever,
From cold mountain springs,
To o'erpersuade the haunted ear
It new-creates the tune it sings.

II

Above Loch Avon

So on we marched. That awful loneliness
Received our souls as air receives the smoke.
Then larger breath we drew, felt years gone by,
And in a new dimension turned and spoke.

III

Loch Avon

Loch A'an, Loch A'an, hoo deep ye lie!
Tell nane yer depth and nane shall I.
Bricht though yer deepmaist pit may be,
Ye'll haunt me till the day I dee.
Bricht, an' bricht, an' bricht as air,
Ye'll haunt me noo for evermair.

IV

Images of beauty and of destruction:
The pool, black as peat, still as a blade.
No man so strong of limb but its current is stronger.

The tarn, luminous verdigris, still as a jewel.
No sound save, once, a thunder of snow from the corrie.
No man so hot of blood but finds death in its water.

Summit of Sgoran Dhu, snow driving dim on the blast.
Far below, Loch Einach, precipice-sided and sombre.
No man so sure of self but here he must tremble.

Here man escapes from the futile sense of safety,
The busy and cheerful acts that invade the soul.
Here the Destroying Angel smites and they fail.

And he knows again the sharpness of life, its balance,
The mind springing and strong poised against danger and pain.
Nothing avails him here but the mind's own fineness.

V

Fires

Firelight: the quiet heart of a little room
Where the lamp burns low and the shadows hover.
Out of the night are we come, where the gathered gloom
Hangs softly now that the wild hill rain is over,
And all that moves—a star or two—moves slowly;
Great clouds plod to the slouch of the wind their drover.

In from the great processional of space,
From the tramp of stars in their careless crossing
Of gulf on infinite gulf, from the foaming race
Where the wind caught at the corries, and the old tossing
Of the fire-tormented rock in the ridge of mountains
Seemed to awake anew in the clouds' new tossing—

In from the cold blown dark: from flame to flame—
From the hidden flame of cosmic motion
That roars through all the worlds and will not tame,
Driving the stars on the crest of its own commotion,
To the little leaping flame that our own hands kindled:
In, as the boats come in from the width of ocean.

Narrow the room is, shut from infinities.
Only the new-lit fire is keeping
Hint of the ancient fire ere the first of days.
And we three talk awhile to the spell of its leaping,
And are silent awhile and talk again and are silent;
And an older fire than the hearth-fire wakes from sleeping—

The fire that smouldering deep in the heart of man
Lies unfelt and forgotten under
Our surface ways, till a swift wind rise and fan
The covered heat to a blaze that snaps asunder

The strange restraints of life for a soaring moment;
And we lift unquiet eyes and stare in wonder

At the infinite reaches the tottering flames reveal,
Watching the high defences crumble
And the walls of our self-seclusion gape and reel,
Till with heart-beat loud as a toppling rampart's grumble
Out from our comforting selves to the ungirt spaces
One with we know not what of desire, we stumble.

VI

There is no merit in speaking the language of the saints when one is a denizen of heaven.

And if upon the angry height
   There comes a golden hour
Of magical and lovely light
   And terrible in power,

That lights the world unto its ends
   As God Himself were by,
And its pure lustre straitly sends
   To the confines of the sky,

Illumining the width of land
   And all the hills that are—
Peak after peak how clear they stand,
   Farther and yet more far,

Till one stands out—O pure surprise!—
   Not visioned in the past,
And men with startled rapturous eyes
   See the unseen at last:

Then ah! if I am walking there,
   And breathe that blue serene,
And see through that enchanted air
   The form of the unseen,

It may be I at last shall know
   A god's experience,
Perceive the world without the show
   That opens to the sense.

The world will stir and undulate
   With meanings missed before,
As up the mountain-slopes in spate
   The startled red-deer pour.

VII

The Hill

So it may be a hill was there,
    Blue, tremulous, afar.
I looked and thought the gleam was air,
    And thought the morning star

Might tremble thus and thus resolve
    Its fire in common light,
Content, while world and sun revolve,
    To vanish from the sight.

So hard it was that morn to tell
    If earth or heaven I saw,
I knew not how on earth to dwell
    Nor how from heaven withdraw.

For vanishing within my thought,
    And stealing back to view,
Earth mingled so with heaven, they wrought
    One universe from two.

VIII

The Hill Burns

So without sediment
Run the clear burns of my country,
Fiercely pure,
Transparent as light
Gathered into its own unity,
Lucent and without colour;
Or green,
Like clear deeps of air,
Light massed upon itself,
Like the green pinions,
Cleaving the trouble of approaching night,
Shining in their own lucency,
Of the great angels that guarded the Mountain;
Or amber so clear
It might have oozed from the crystal trunk
Of the tree Paradisal,
Symbol of life,
That grows in the presence of God eternally.
And these pure waters
Leap from the adamantine rocks,
The granites and schists
Of my dark and stubborn country.
From gaunt heights they tumble,
Harsh and desolate lands,
The plateau of Braeriach
Where even in July
The cataracts of wind
Crash in the corries with the boom of seas in anger;
And Corrie Etchachan
Down whose precipitous
Narrow defile

Thunder the fragments of rock
Broken by winter storms
From their aboriginal place;
And Muich Dhui's summit,
Rock defiant against frost and the old grinding of ice,
Wet with the cold fury of blinding cloud,
Through which the snow-fields loom up, like ghosts from a world of eternal annihilation,
And far below, where the dark waters of Etchachan are wont to glint,
An unfathomable void.
Out of these mountains,
Out of the defiant torment of Plutonic rock,
Out of fire, terror, blackness and upheaval,
Leap the clear burns,
Living water,
Like some pure essence of being,
Invisible in itself,
Seen only by its movement.

IX

The three great rocks of Beinn Mheadhoin
    Behind, the sunset gleaming.
Their shadows on the light are cast
    Like smoke from bonfires streaming.

What strange complicity of earth
    With what bright god is here,
That she may lay her mark on heaven
    And light be marked by her?

So filled is all her heart with light,
    Her valleys and ravines,
She takes his nature on herself,
    But knows not what it means.

For all the air is tinged with earth
    Through which his glory shone,
And he, whose passage is the air,
    Must put her nature on.

O purest light, on whom may lie
    No shadow of a shade,
On thee, for sign of love to earth,
    Those three dark bands are laid.

X

The Bush

In that pure ecstasy of light
The bush is burning bright.
Its substance is consumed away
And only form doth stay,
Form as of boughs, but boughs of fire,
That flicker and aspire,
Or stand in stilled beatitude
And shine, which is their good.
So holy Sun, pour down on me,
That I pure fight may be.
Thy life, my form—a whole unique
Whereof I would not speak,
But only be't, that thou mayst shine
In this new shape of thine.

XI

Lux Perpetua
Nobis cum semel occidit brevis lux . . .

A sweep of sky went round and round the place;
    The land ran sloping away to the left and right,
And the hills looked low across that width of space,
    The sea, blue-white.

O clarity, colour, the height of a winter noon,
    The flocking of stormy gulls in the stormy sky,
The flocking of winds together, the flight, the croon
    Of their passing by,

And a hush behind them that lay on the wood like a spell,
    A hush that was quick with the underthrob of sound.
After, to south-south-west through asphodel
    The sun slid round.

Last, the dark; and out of the jewel-blue east
    Sudden the first full star, the oft-approved,
That with the tranquil motion of a priest,
    Somewhat removed

Above the restless turmoil earth must know,
    Gazing through clear aerial lucency,
Looks on the face of light, until the glow
    Perceptibly

Shines from his own devoted countenance;
    So mediates the evening star, so keeps
The sun, and prophesies the lights that glance
    Through vaster deeps.

And we returning take the star of eve,
    We mortal and our sun how soon gone down,
For proclamation and thereby believe
    The wild renown

Of life whose long potentialities
    Quicken, like flame from perishing star to star
Through unimagined primal silences
    And vaults afar,

New revelations of the only Light,
    Illumining awhile, again returning
Within the unbroken splendour infinite,
    The always burning.

XII

Strange gifts of pleasure has the mind,
Strange darknesses the soul.
An influence takes her from the blind
Dark worlds that round her roll—

The world of rocks and streaming seas,
And thrusting tangled roots;
Of bogs and old engulfèd trees,
And boulders dank as brutes.

And sunken there the mind may not
Relume her former fire,
All her bright pinnacles forgot,
Her vehemence and ire.

Down and down and further down,
De-formed, annulled, unmade,
She feels the whole creation drown,
The ache of form allayed.

The streaming seas, the ocean gulf,
The rocks, dissolve away.
Now she may re-create herself.
Now is the primal day.

XIII

Tread not in the planets' places,
    Follow not the sun,
Fear the empyrean spaces,
Heavenly ardour see thou shun.

When the companies of morning
    Sing in starry quire,
Turn thou back with sound and scorning,
Lest thou hearken and desire.

Dayspring for thee no more be haunted,
    Birds flute in vain,
Mazed thou shalt hear young April vaunted,
Wind in the leaves, and summer rain.

Love in the dim moist wood appal thee,
    Unholy to thee still;
And voices of thy friends that call thee
Faint and faintlier echo will,

Crying: O lost! O lost for ever!
    Deluded and beguiled!
Crying: The peak! The peak! Ah never!
Crying: O cold and cold and wild!

XIV

Blackbird in Snow

O that early morning fluting,
   Rising tranquil through the snow!
Tranquil, did I say? That rapture?
   Those ecstatic thrills?—Ah, no.

All too short and too uncertain
   Is the blackbird's time of song.
A few brief months to sing in, out of
   Years as brief is not so long

Each bird in turn may learn the music
   That has no measurement in time,
But whoso hears one note has hearkened
   Already an eternal chime.

The blackbird's song with love is shaken
   And madness of approaching doom,
Delirious desire to capture
   All passion in a little room.

And yet, that note! There was no passion.
   Too clear it welled, too absolute.
No bird of earth, that soon must perish,
   Sounded that wise and lonely flute.

Rather, it seemed, the silver singing
   Echoed—remote, contained, and pure—
From some keen order of existence
   Whereof we are but rarely sure;

Unseen, unheard, yet all beside us,
   And co-existent with our own,
That shines through ours at quickened moments
   Like light through lovely forms of stone,

Making the marble goddess tremble,
   All soft and luminous, and live
With an intenser life than even
   Her rapt creator knew to give.

So sometimes through our common being
   That keener mode of life may shine,
And eye may see, and ear may hearken,
   In mortal forms an air divine.

Unprophesied, to-day, to-morrow,
   The things I touch, the things I see,
In flame of that fierce life supernal
   Burn to their own identity.

It is, it is, the blackbird singing!
   The beat of time is in the note.
Yet its own infinite arises
   From that small perishable throat.

XV

Summit of Corrie Etchachan

But in the climbing ecstasy of thought,
Ere consummation, ere the final peak,
Come hours like this. Behind, the long defile,
The steep rock-path, alongside which, from under
Snow-caves, sharp-corniced, tumble the ice-cold waters.
And now, here, at the corrie's summit, no peak,
No vision of the blue world, far, unattainable,
But this grey plateau, rock-strewn, vast, silent,
The dark loch, the toiling crags, the snow;
A mountain shut within itself, yet a world,
Immensity. So may the mind achieve,
Toiling, no vision of the infinite,
But a vast, dark and inscrutable sense
Of its own terror, its own glory and power.

XVI

Its own most lovely wraith the tree
In its own form hath now displayed.
Bright boughs of heaven are not more free,
That of pure life are fashionèd.

And I am free who saw the wraith,
Since only undistracted eyes
May pierce the myriad dreams of faith
And view the tree without disguise.

XVII

Quiet over Lochnagar
    Hung the afterglow,
And the burning western star
    In its element did go.

But eastward stacked and riven there stood
    Ramparts of angry air,
As though the crag's similitude
    Were risen to front it there.

For light in light will move, and pain
    Find pain's dark phantasy,
And all things to their like pertain
    And seek their own degree.

And everywhere the burning mind
    In rapt and grave surprise
The secret stigma of its kind
    May learn to recognise.

XVIII

Caul', caul' as the wall
That rins frae under the snaw
On Ben a' Bhuird,
And fierce, and bricht,
This water's nae for ilka mou',
But him that's had a waucht or noo,
Nae wersh auld waters o' the plain
Can sloke again,
But aye he clim's the weary heicht
To fin' the wall that loups like licht,
Caulder than mou' can thole, and aye
The warld cries oot on him for fey.

Wall, well. *Wersh*, tasteless.
Waught, draught. *Thole*, endure.

XIX

Fawn

But in what mood
Of dreaming quietude
That thought came leaping like a startled fawn
To lose itself in covert of the wood—
I know not, but remember that I stood,
Silent as one may stand at dawn,
Breath hardly drawn,
And eyes intent
To hold yet longer in the firmament
The pure essential star:
So lost I, so recovered, that fair fawn.
But could not wait,
Seeing it there afar,
So plain,
So still and straight,
But followed fleet,
If haply I might meet
The golden flash of that fair thought again;
But saw it melt within my mind,
And might not find
A trace of it where'er I turned my feet.
O delicate!
The slender limb, the flight of fire,
The vanishing of that which does not go,
The morning star within my shaken brain,
My world a-tremble with a new desire,
Dwelt-in by life I may not fully know.

XX

Spring

But still I must remember how the sound
Of waters echoed in my ear all night,
How fitfully I slumbered, waked, and found
The singing burns, the cataracts, the might

Of tumults drunken with the melting snow,
Filling the starry darkness with their joy;
And heard the singing stars, that paused to know
What shout was that? what rapture, "Spring, ahoy!"

XXI

The Flooded Meads

The flooded meads! I gazed on them with wonder,
Remembering the snows whose winter-long
Abiding on the mountains now was over.
      Powerful and strong
      The loosened waters throng.

Strange to the heart as the waters that brim the valley
Thronging the loosened words pour down at last,
Born of what antique storm the glad world cares not,
      That from the past
      Takes but the song it cast.

Flood

The pools came over the brim at night,
    And the river silently
Glided up with a fierce delight
To the tall bank where the willows were white
    And the primrose roots lay.

And O but the unsubstantial blue
    That the earth was at dawn!
And how the sober flats grew
Elfin, uncertain, half like dew
    And half like light withdrawn.

And all of a sudden the world was strange
    With the strangeness of things that seem
More familiar the more they change,
Like the queer, familiar forms that range
    Through the wide lands of dream.

XXIII

Pool Beside the Birches

Pool, where would thy waters run,
Fleeing so fast toward the sun?
Dost thou not know thou art shut in?
Thou canst not pass thy boundary,
And 'tis but air that hurries by,
Disturbing thy serenity.
Does the heavenly mystery prove
So urgent thou canst not but move
In emulation of its flight
As it speeds onward to the light?
Or hast thou purpose of thine own
To us, as to the wind, unknown?

XXIV

Day Without Sun

Now the radiance is gone.
Cold is all I look upon.
Each curve and contour of the hill,
Houses and bridges, dyke and mill,
Every branch and twig and stone,
Stands out separate, alone,
This winter clarity compelling
Each to its own single telling.
The world that hung, a globe of light,
Consorting with the planets bright,
Like them reflecting back the sun
In still unbroken benison,
Now is only earth again,
Her high destiny mista'en.
—Or is it that she may not stay
Too long in that bright company,
Lest all her life be turned to flame
And she be nothing but a name,
Burning unquenchably serene
With high apocalyptic mien,
Suffused with light until the glow
Is all of her that one may know?
—And so, to keep her earthly grace,
She draws a cloud before her face?

XXV

A Girl in Love

Until the sun of thy desire
Shone on the girl and made her glow
And turned her movement into fire,
Her glance to light, we did not know

How fair she was, nor how her ways
That we had thought dull earth, could burn,
And match with those bright heresies
That earth to seeming fire can turn.

Surprise a movement quick like flame—
'Tis she, her thoughts wheel on the wing.
Her woods are shapes of fire, her frame
Is haloed with a fiery ring.

Her rocks, her hills, are kindled now.
Her nature and thy light combine,
And manifold in her art thou,
Her loveliness a part of thine.

XXVI

Embodiment

Light swum between the mountains
That glowed themselves like light.
Light was the principle of their making
And light their substance.

Not out of chaos
Were wrought the cankered bosses,
The jags, splinters, screes, peat-hags,
The runkled laps and clefts.

For light, like every stuff
That a creator uses,
Must jag and splinter, thwart and tangle,
Ere the vision be embodied.

There is no substance but light.
The visible worlds
Are light
Undergoing process of creation

Into some vision
That a god thought out in light
And that in consummation
Will shine as pure light.

We are this substance.
We are too near it,
As the god wrests it and strains it,
To see it for what it is.

We are the knots and tangles
In a god's vision,
The thrawn refusals
Of material to become form.

But if, being ourselves light,
Having in us the principle of making,
We create ourselves in a form
Imagined in no god's mind,

Will that also in consummate being
Shine as pure light,
Like the shining sides of Glen Guisachan,
Wet with storm,

That shine now like light uncreated,
Pure, a primal essence unconditioned to form,
A thought still in a god's mind,
And yet there, meeting the eye, in the form of the gullies
  we love?

XXVII

O licht amo' the hills,
S'uld ye gang oot,
To whatna dark the warld'll fa'.

Nae mair the thochts o' men
'll traivel 'yont the warld
Frae aff some shinin' Ben.

Nae mair the glint o' snaw
Oot ower the warld's wa'
'll mak men doot
Gin they've their e'en or na.

O licht amo' the hills!

OTHER LYRICS

Crusoe

The spirit roves through vastness of its own,
In turmoil or dead waters; oft alone
It founders where the hungry reefs are strown.

There may it chance upon a quiet isle,
The dew of thought unbrushed from mile on mile,
Thought that had known the primal dusk awhile.

How shall it run rejoicing to explore
Woodland and corrie echoing to the roar
Of streams that from their mountain gorges pour!

Up to the blue escarpments of the hills,
In intimate league with the elusive rills,
How shall it climb through every way it wills!

Yet shall there come a sail: impatient years
Recall us to forgotten toil and tears.
Our thought strays thither as the low wind veers.

The Man who Journeyed to his Heart's Desire

He journeyed east, he journeyed west,
Ever he sought one perfect rest,
Ever the moon and the stars gleamed cold,
But the moon was withered, the years were old,
Ere he came to the land of the Weary Blest.

And there the folk who had sought as he
Stared in a silence stonily
(For nothing was even worth a sigh)
On the long straight line of the sea and sky,
And the long straight line of the sand and the sea.

Winter Branches

Against the smoke-browned wall
The browner winter branches
Stand out hardly at all;
They do not tremble in the misty evening.

But under the open sky
Where the stars in clear and tranquil
Sufficiency go by,
They leap up quivering into the vastness

Like flame, like the thought of man
Leaping from earth's nurture,
Through span on alien span,
To tremble around the stars its kindred.

Astonishment is in the Skies

Astonishment is in the skies;
The gliding waters murmur o'er
Songs that are their own surprise;
The trees ne'er looked like this before.

Thine is the ravishment they wear.
I turn from thee in such content
That where I go thou still art there,
And all the world with thee is blent.

Creation of an Earth

So com'st thou on me, O my star?
Too near, too near, though still afar.
And must I journey on to thee
That our convergence speedier be?
Now, now, ah, headlong let me fall
And burn in thee at once for all!
—But no, not yet absolved am I:
Thou'rt still without, still drawing nigh.
I mount, I yearn, I feel thy force
Like dissolution strike my course...
...And now far off thou travellest on,
Gone by, gone past recall, quite gone.
And I must hold my way through space,
Nor drop from my accustomed place,
I torn, I plundered, I undone.

Even so, they swear, spoke once the sun.

A Dead Love

The snow has fallen, our love is stripped and cold.
But there, far in, deep in the secret grove,
Snow lights the branch—each bough and twig is strown—
Like the X-Ray that penetrates to the bone.

So in this winter blight I pierce your soul.
The sacred wood, dark to me heretofore,
Is now revealed. We need no longer grope.
Each sees the other, without desire or hope.

Without Expiation

So this inexpiable wrong
Remains between us. Let it bide.
Nor add the further wrong to say
It taught us much, or, *humbles pride,*

Or, *proved a blessing in the end.*
For these are lies. 'Tis unredeemed:
Pure pain, pure loss, destructive, sore,
And ugly as at first it seemed.

Well, let us recognize the thing:
No reparation can be made.
Put all pretence away, and meet
The consequences unafraid.

If fear devitalised us then,
The easy comfort to allow
'Tis not so bad as once we thought
Will not devitalise us now.

Ptolemaic System of Love

So, my first love, the time is o'er
When even regret we need explore.
No radiance moves between us now:
What then? We were not less aglow.
Blind, frenzied, faulty, though our mood,
It yet had its beatitude,
And taught us one approach to bliss
That happier loves than ours may miss.
As errors of the mind may grace
With their own gleam the heavenly place,
The stations of the stars beguile
To their own patterns for awhile,
And lighten with a new intent
The all-sufficient firmament,
So, though in terror we descry
A deep and ever deepening sky,
And know our ancient love is vain,
Proved false, ne'er to be truth again,
Because it once was truth for us,
Heaven let itself be measured thus.
—Yet oh! farewell—that deepening sky
Reminds me thou must further fly.
Star from its neighbour star is hurled,
And vaster wheels the expanding world.
What stature, ah, what love shall be
Equal to this immensity?

FOURTEEN YEARS

Snow

I did not know. How could I understand,
   I, who had scorned the very name of love?
   Clear were my eyes and heaven was clear above;
Clarity held the long lines of the land;
Hill after hill raced proud at my demand.
   Too careless to be triumphant, O enough
   Of triumph had I who knew the transience of
Clear cloud and wind: clear colour; earth blown and
   tanned.

And now—and now—I am mazed to find my world
   Sore altered in the passing of a night
(And never a dream all night had round me curled)
   No sound, no proclamation, no delight
Of haunting prophecy came, no hurricane swirled.
   But at morn the earth was strange, a blur, white.

La Vita Nuova

   I have been dumb these many days since knowing
     The power of that which once I did deride.
   I have been dumb because you took my pride
Broke it and gave me back new-forged and glowing,
And took my deep humility unshowing
     Before the curious world and let it bide,
     No more a hidden thing that would not hide,
And marred my will and made it strong for going.

Surely, O love, supreme as very death,
    Closing a whole experience for aye,
      Love takes the unbribed soul; and hauntings of
Its dark finality disturb the breath,
    Till love itself proclaim delivery
      From the last cowardice, the fear of love.

Half Love

No, love me not: not on my hungry breast,
    Nor mouth, nor mouth by your mouth made aware,
    Not on my pulses' tumult, not my hair,
Not on my body be your love confessed.
But still by eager thought be I caressed,
    Trouble me still with longing, love from far,
    Still be to me the burning of a star
In heaven perceived but yet on earth possessed.

So coward I cried, broken and spent with loving,
    Broken and spent with half-fulfilled desire.
I am too weak and mortal for your having
    Who fear to flare not burnish in your fire.
O star, O star from utmost heaven removing,
    How can I hold you in my arms entire?

In Separation

So take my love. Transmute it how you will.
   It passes from me and is mine no more.
   My insufficiency is not in store
Of love, but in the dark and subtle skill
Of alchemy, and idly I fulfil
   The law of love who simple love outpour,
   Till you, receiving me within your door,
Alter my gift. So take. Redeem me still.

For though all labour, all I struggle for,
   Be sacramental of my love for you,
     Bearing its essence, so I am not spent.
But swift and eager, a strong inquisitor
   Within your secretest pulse, my love throbs through,
     Too instant to attend on sacrament.

Without my Right

By longing I could draw thee from the deep
   Of that far country whence am I recluse,
     Claiming thy substance for my proper use,
Importunate against thee even in sleep.
What then? Shalt thou be raided, I to creep
   Thieving within thy self, and introduce
     The subtle languor of brain and limb fallen loose
That follows ravished essence? hold thee so cheap?

Love, love, I have no mind for sane respect.
   I crave too long thy presence to abhor
     For thee rape's dark dishonour. Without my right
I draw thee on toward me and infect
   My being with thine. And through the monstrous night
     Rages within me quintessential war.

Love Eternal

There are two ways of loving. One must own:
   Jealous, exclusive, careless of the event,
   Abandoned, rash, superbly insolent,
That having has the world and to atone
For theft so huge, were other worlds but known
   Would have them too in having its content;
   That having not has all of punishment,
Yet will not have except it have alone.

And one is free and unconcerned as air
   Or subtle ether or the wash of light.
It seeketh not but is already there,
     Nor knoweth absence more than doth the sound
   Of waters from their movement, though all night
     It flee through space, they rove upon the ground.

An Ecstasy Remembered

The shining moment of our ecstasy,
   Static in memory now, uneased, unmarred,
   Too sheer, too sharp, too adamantine hard
For even time to take its edge away.
Time, that involves all old experience
   In the eternal flux, until at last
   It alters the unalterable past,
Leaves this its adamant, compressed, intense.

A shining group, the bare wet birches stood,
   Their trunks like glass, their thousand rain-drop caught
Like crystal globes fine cut on crystal wood,
   As though from one pure crystal all were wrought:
   So crystal-hard, fine cut in crystal thought,
Our moment of amazed beatitude.

Growth

This bitter wisdom is my strength to-night,
   That only things safe and mechanical
   Achieve the end fore-vaunted, and forestall
Their own defeat; and still are in the right,
Wrong not and are not wronged, but keep their state.
   And loving has no safety, none, no charm
   Against the astonishment and quick alarm
Of life incalculable and elate.

So may I blunt the sharpness of my sore.
   I had not failed you had you been the same
   As that old self that at my bidding came
     In dream and memory; but now—but now—
Anguished I break the vows I never swore
     And bear the shame for deeds I disallow.

Pardon

I did not dream you would forgive me thus.
   O God ! that wrestling through the bitter night,
   Both holding fast, yet maimed, exhausted quite,
And after, no beatitude for us,
But hatred, shame, contempt, disgust, despair,
   Estrangement and unsanctified remorse
   And black self-knowledge, eating like a curse.
And now, your pardon—and that look—that air.

Once in strange seas at dawn I saw an isle
   Soar into cloud, then caught my breath—there hung
     On upper air a peak pellucid, blue,
   Stilled to eternal form; within me sprung
Eternal recognition. So your smile.
   Go now, or stay. I have the whole of you.

Not in a Glass

Let us have done with image. For the light
    Shines only, though its shining be divine,
    It has no mode of being save to shine.
You are not thus who live in your own right.
And air is urgent, else the life is spent,
    And yet I am not dead apart from you.
    Stars keep their orbit, which you cannot do,
Nor is our union flame, nor waters blent.

But stark we stand beyond the veils of speech,
    I AM for each of us the ultimate fate,
Betrayed, betraying, broken each for each,
    I taking you, you me, accepting doom
Of what we are, and yet—O profligate!—
    More than we are we give, and more resume.

Real Presence

Clear as the endless ecstasy of stars
   That mount for ever on an intense air;
   Or running pools, of water cold and rare,
In chiselled gorges deep amid the scaurs,
So still, the bright dawn were their best device,
   Yet like a thought that has no end they flow;
   Or Venus, when her white unearthly glow
Sharpens like awe on skies as green as ice:

To such a clearness love is come at last,
   Not disembodied, transubstantiate,
      But substance and its essence now are one;
   And love informs, yet is the form create.
No false gods now, the images o'ercast,
   We are love's body, or we are undone.

OTHER POEMS

Achiltibuie

Here on this edge of Europe I stand on the edge of being.
Floating on light isle after isle takes wing.
Burning blue are the peaks, rock that is older than thought,
And the sea burns blue—or is it the air between—
They merge, they take one another upon them.
I have fallen through time and found the enchanted world.
Where all is beginning.
The obstinate rocks
Are a fire of blue, a pulse of power, a beat
In energy, the sea dissolves
And I too melt, am timeless, a pulse of light.

Next Morning

This morning the rocks are adamant—we knew they were—
Monsters, planting their feet against the gale.
The bright sea is itself, and could be no other,
Sharp and hard, cavorting and lashing its tail.

A world in active mood, knowing the grammar of now,
The present tense, a fierce exultation of act,
No meanings that cannot be shouted, no faith but is based
On the tough, the mendacious intractable splendour of fact.

On a Still Morning

I hear the silence now.
Alive within its heart
Are the sounds that can not be heard
That the ear may not dispart?

As white light gathers all—
The rose and the amethyst,
The ice-green and the copper-green,
The peacock blue and the mist—

So if I bend my ear
To silence, I grow aware
The stir of sounds I have almost heard
That are not quite there.

Rhu Coigach
A headland on the Atlantic

Thrusting at me the gaunt rocks cry:
This is the end, there is nothing further to know,
Here is the last foothold, the whelming wave is beyond
There is no more for the mind to undergo.

But the rocks lie: there is negation to undergo
To know oneself blank, blind, worthless, rejected, done,
A stranger in the outwash of a bitter sea.
This too must be apprehended, its savour won.

Falketind

With cruel beak and one black pinion spread,
Scourging the sky, the Falcon mountain towers,
Fierce to be free of heaven, doomed to be rock,
Type of our own accursed agonizing,
Wrestling with gods for nights that are not ours,
Man's doom prefigured, his absolution wrought.
Through his eyes he is absolved, his climbing feet,
Through the long halt, gazing, the breath caught,
On that black sweep of wing, that lifted head.

The Trees

Forgotten temples in forgotten lands,
Half quarried stone forbidden to achieve
The form some master-thought had asked to leave
Cut on it—and reflected there it stands,
Lichened and frustrate—columns that the sands
Have long since gulfed and cities that the heave
Of earth's cramped body carelessly did thieve
Of fame, and halls both raided and ruined by hands:

All these I thought on—all the dead done world,
Deliberate things and things without desire.
For it was April, and I dared not look
Save furtively upon the trees, that whirled
And fled and followed my path. And one was fire,
One mocked; one melted while I swore she shook.

Underground

What passionate tumult tore this black disturbance
Out of the rugged heart of the obstinate rock,
Fixing secure a thousand-age-old shock
Beneath the quiet country's imperturbance,
I have no wit to utter, nor what breath
Blew like a bubble that flees through water this
Chasm in the bowels of earth where dark streams kiss
In guilty dark slant shores they will kiss till death

And never look on: but I give my thanks
Tonight to that antique destructive whim
That so the risen and torrential flood
That else had burst all measure and drowned the banks
And swamped my life, may pour along those grim
And secret caves, and none discern its thud.

The Dryad

So faunus leaped: and she, caught unaware,
Flung back one wild glance at her tree, and spoke
No word, nor shrieked, but desperately broke
From his embrace; recaptured from the snare
Broke twice, and thrice: the fourth time mute despair
Shackled her limbs. She drooped. But he could cloak
Lust in rare beauty and of the brutal folk
She too was born. She laughed and yielded there.

And after all, why flee?—since not in flight
Is there escape for her from tyrant earth.
Her flickering limbs that flare and flash from sight
Are scarce her own, but through the flickering boughs
Must melt, and she be captive to the mirth,
Snatched by the faun or not, of earth's carouse.

Arthur's Seat
Early Morning

That summer night a haze of apricot
    Drifted about the spires and houses. Low
    And luminous it hung, and in the glow
The city trembled, like a thing half-wrought
From dreams and wild desire, that ere the thought
    Took substance faded, till it seemed to grow
    Part of the very sky, and none might know
The earth from heaven. Dusk quivered. Dark shook them not.

And we at morning found the city lying,
    And a flash of sea and the mountains-line afar,
    Gathered in awful trance: and watched it broken:
But kept, while earth, indifferent and flying,
    Danced on through heaven like any other star,
    One still rapt secret way of hers for token.

The Burning Glass

Be not my burning-glass! O love, I fear.
    The low faint star, blue of the thunder-haze,
    Blurred water-pools — the beauty of them dismays
My senses, that hold precariously dear
Loveliness that defeats them. Year by year
    I clutch the radiance by scattered rays,
    Dreaming till death of one proud fusèd blaze,
The revelation, earth's beauty caught and clear.

And now knowing thee I tremble with fear that thou
    Utter the secret word that clarifies.
O, I could watch my world blaze up and perish
As price of that dread knowledge! Yet, not now:
    And be not thou the glass: lest I must cherish
    More than thyself the word that makes thee wise.

Union

Dear, I have not kept back, though I made my boast,
Once, to have dark reserves and hidden store
Of mine own intimate self: but now no more
I am afraid to offer the uttermost
And come all naked to thee: yet thou Know'st
Though more, still less of me than e'er before.
Seeing that the giver gives and the gift is o'er.
But when giver and gift are one, to the end thou ow'st.

Ah love, surrender could not be more complete!
But in the very surrender I discover
New intimacies to show to thee my love
And showing, yet newer privacies secrete,
Till ever upon the marge of oneness we hover,
Yet ever, O love, from lonelier travelling meet.

Street Urchins

In dim green summer silence the woodland
    Lay and I with it, through the afternoon;
And the dusk of pine and the flicker of rowan
    And great curved ferns resolved themselves into a tune

That swayed about me and sung and trembled,
    And died as the long soft whirr of the wind had died
Leaving the dream-deep woodland shadow
    Lax as the tumbled down where the wild duck cried:

Till far off somewhere a rout of urchins
    Raised a clamour, nearer and yet more near,
That sank, and I saw them break toward the open,
    Under the branch-work, a moment, swift and clear,

Bearing each in his hands uprightly
    A green courageous clump of ferns that tossed
Their swooping fronds up on to the shoulders
    Of the running bearers as one by one they crossed,

Like an age-old sculpture suddenly living,
    A processional rite toward the very feet of the god.
Solemn and old and in triumph eternal,
    Earth offering earth, from earth, from the treader the trod.

And forever now on the wood's blurred margin,
    The frieze of pattering boys for me is hung,
Binding the sacrificial ages:
    Till the slow substantial wood where songs are sung

At idle whiles by the crisp or rainy
    Wind, and where glancing light and live things go,
Drifts like a ghostly dream about me,
    Unstable, insecure, a quivering show.

Notes to the Foreword

Warm thanks are due for various kinds of help in the writing of this foreword to Peter Davidson, Victoria McArthur, Helen Mort and Kirk Watson. I am grateful to the Trustees of the National Library of Scotland, to Dairmid Gunn for permission to quote from unpublished letters, and to the Nan Shepherd Estate for their support. I have not supplied specific page references when quoting from *In The Cairngorms,* so all un-referenced quotations should be assumed to have their origins there. Other sources for quoted material are given below.

1   letter from Nan Shepherd to Neil Gunn, 14th March 1930, Deposit 209, Box 19, Folder 7, National Library of Scotland, Edinburgh.
2   letter from Nan Shepherd to Neil Gunn, 2nd April 1931, Deposit 209, Box 19, Folder 7, National Library of Scotland, Edinburgh.
3   *The Living Mountain* (Edinburgh: Canongate, 2011 [first published 1977]), hereafter TLM, p. 23.
4   TLM, p. 108.
5   TLM, p. 9.
6   TLM, p. 2.
7   TLM, p. 12.
8   anon., quoted in Louise Donald, 'Nan Shepherd', *Leopard Magazine,* (October 1977), 20–22, 21.
9   Nan Shepherd, quoted in Louise Donald, 'Nan Shepherd', 20.
10 Louise Donald, 'Nan Shepherd'.
11 Nan Shepherd, quoted in Vivienne Forrest, 'In Search of Nan Shepherd', *Leopard Magazine* (December 1986–January 1987), 17–19, 17.

12   Jessie Kesson, quoted in Vivienne Forrest, 'In Search of Nan Shepherd', 19.
13   Ali Smith, 'Shepherd, Anna (1893–1981)', *Oxford Dictionary of National Biography*, (Oxford University Press, 2004).
14   Nan Shepherd, quoted in Vivienne Forrest, 'In Search of Nan Shepherd', 18.
15   Vivienne Forrest, 'In Search of Nan Shepherd', 17.
16   Jessie Kesson, quoted in Vivienne Forrest, 'In Search of Nan Shepherd', 19.
17   TLM, p. 8.
18   TLM, p. 105.
19   Nan Shepherd, introduction to Charles Murray, *Last Poems* (Aberdeen: Charles Murray Trust/Aberdeen University Press, 1970).
20   Nan Shepherd, quoted in Vivienne Forrest, 'In Search of Nan Shepherd', 19.

The publishers thank Robert Macfarlane for his considerable help in making the new edition of *In the Cairngorms* possible, as well as Erlend Clouston, Nan's literary trustee, for entrusting Galileo with this project. Thanks also to Charlotte Peacock, George Allan, June Allan and Sandy McIntosh.

All the poems included in this book are published by arrangement with the Nan Shepherd Estate, and have been published previously, either in *In The Cairngorms* or in *Wild Geese: A Collection of Nan Shepherd's Writing*. This is the first time they have been collected in one volume.